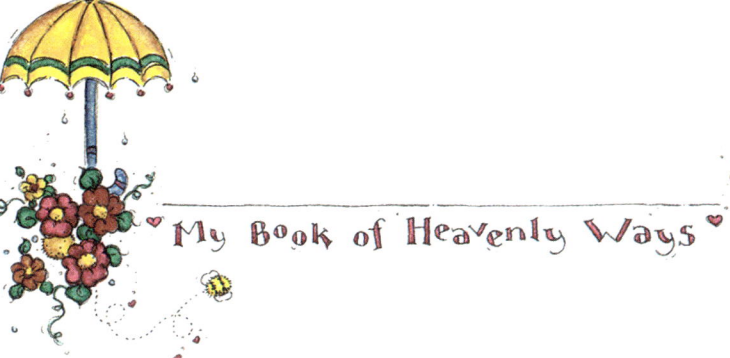

My Book of Heavenly Ways

About the Artist

Deb Haas Abell lives with her husband and two children in a cozy home with a picket fence, nestled in a small town in Southern Indiana. She hopes this book will put you in touch with heavenly help and healing...and the angel in you!

About the Author

Molly Wigand lives in suburban Kansas City with her husband and three angelic sons. She's grateful to be able to share her inner angel's thoughts and feelings with you.

Heavenly Ways to Heal from Grief and Loss

Created and Illustrated by
Deb Haas Abell

Written by
Molly Wigand

Text © 1998 by Molly Wigand
Art © 1998 by Deb Haas Abell
Published by One Caring Place
Abbey Press
St. Meinrad, Indiana 47577

All rights reserved.
No part of this book may be used or reproduced in any manner
without written permission of the publisher, except in the case
of brief quotations embodied in critical articles and reviews.

Library of Congress Catalog Number 98-72644

ISBN 0-87029-319-2

Printed in the United States of America

Grief ~ and the Angel in You

Losing someone we love is among the most painful experiences human beings endure. Thankfully, each of us has help to guide us on our journey through grief.

One "helper" we all have is an "inner angel," inspiring us in our time of loss.

May this book help you to hear your angel's message of calm assurance: You are not alone. God's love and compassion are with you each step of the way.

Feel free to jot your thoughts and feelings on the write-on activity pages or, if you prefer, keep your reflections privately in your heart.

May your angel guide you from grief to grace.

Light and Life

Faith Joy Hope

The pain of losing someone close is one of the most heartrending experiences anyone can endure. Grief challenges you to believe in the healing power of God.

Count on your inner angel to hold your hand, to illuminate your darkest moments, to return God's peace to your life. Your heavenly reserve of strength and love will help to ease the burden you bear.

Harmony

Charity

Grace and Goodness

The Many Faces of Grief

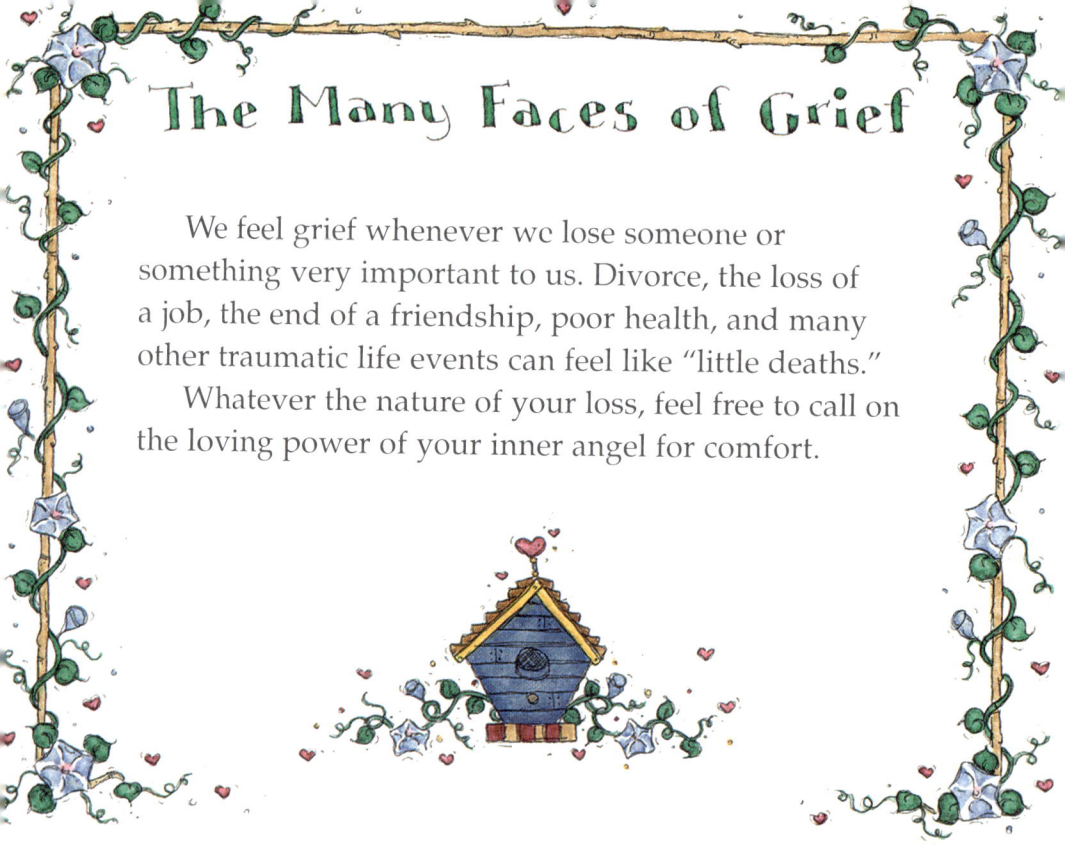

We feel grief whenever we lose someone or something very important to us. Divorce, the loss of a job, the end of a friendship, poor health, and many other traumatic life events can feel like "little deaths."

Whatever the nature of your loss, feel free to call on the loving power of your inner angel for comfort.

The Art of Healing

♥ Previous to this loss, what was the biggest hurt you've experienced in your life?

♥ How did you recover from that loss? What helped you heal?

Faith

Love Hurts

As with physical wounds, healing from grief takes time. You may feel overwhelmed by many difficult emotions. You may be angry, in shock, lonely. You may have trouble sleeping or eating. Simple tasks can seem like huge hurdles. You may wonder if your life will ever feel "normal" again.

Just as we have been given the capacity to love and be loved, we have received the ability to heal when we lose someone we love. Ask your inner angel to help you trust in God's healing power.

My Loved One's at Peace, But What About Me?

Well-meaning friends may tell you not to grieve, reminding you that your loved one is "better off."

Chances are, it's difficult to find comfort in that promise right now. Though you realize your loved one is at peace, your own human feelings of loneliness, loss, and sorrow remain.

The Healing Power of Tears

♥ It's tempting to hide or push aside grief, believing that if you ignore the pain, it will go away. Yet the only way past pain is through it, embracing all the emotions you feel. Is there a special friend you can trust to listen to your feelings?

♥ Set aside some crying time. Though the sadness and tears may seem unbearable, they are necessary parts of healing.

Everybody's Different

Don't try to compare your grief with other people's. Each person's grief has its own dimensions and color and shape.

If people close to you are grieving in a way you don't understand or appreciate, be tolerant. Realize they are doing the best they can to heal and move on.

Grieving people, understandably, can be sensitive and impatient. Your inner angel can help you to be extra forgiving and understanding at this painful time.

Express Yourself

You may feel angry or disappointed with God, thinking your loved one's life should have been spared. You may think God has deserted you, leaving you ill-equipped to deal with your loss. Try to remember that God is not punishing you. God suffers with you in your loss and wants you to find healing.

Acknowledge your honest feelings toward God without guilt or shame. Your inner angel can help you to accept your emotions as normal and natural.

♥ How do you feel toward God right now? Write a letter expressing your doubts and fears.

Dear God...

Grace

For the Good Times ~

Remembering parts of your loved one's life may be painful right after your loss occurs. But, in time, you'll be able to focus beyond sadness on the precious legacy of memories and good feelings left behind.

When you feel ready, call on your inner angel to help you remember the happy times. Each memory you recall makes it a little easier to be thankful for your loved one's life and to carry on.

Let Peace Begin with Me

It's not uncommon to feel some guilt or resentment when a loved one dies. We may even feel angry with him or her for dying.

And, while we may have many wonderful memories, chances are that the relationship also included some difficult moments. These ups and downs are natural in genuine, loving relationships.

Let your inner angel help you identify and accept your feelings. Know that God understands your struggles and will help you find peace of mind.

Bless Your Memories

♥ List three special memories of your loved one. How did he or she make those memories special?

♥ Write to your loved one about something you regret. Ask God to bring peace and forgiveness to this hurting place in your heart.

Speed Bumps

Some emotional moments may catch you off guard, bringing waves of sorrow to your heart. "Happy times" like holidays and anniversaries can be acutely painful. You may feel especially sad on your loved one's birthday and the first anniversary of your loss.

Be patient with yourself and realize that waves of grief may come more frequently at emotional times of the year. Allow your inner angel to help you plan your holidays, setting aside special "remembering times" to spend in thought with your loved one.

Set aside special "Remembering Times"

Anniversaries

Holidays

Birthdays

Comforting Rituals

Some mourners feel the urge to discard all of a loved one's belongings, thinking this will ward off painful memories. Other people "enshrine" the one who is gone, keeping whole rooms and closets intact.

If possible, avoid either of these extremes. With God's help, you can choose meaningful keepsakes of your loved one's life to remind you of the happiness your relationship has brought through the years.

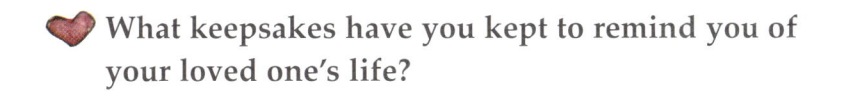

♥ What keepsakes have you kept to remind you of your loved one's life?

♥ What ceremonies and rituals have helped you heal from your grief?

Remember the happiness you shared.

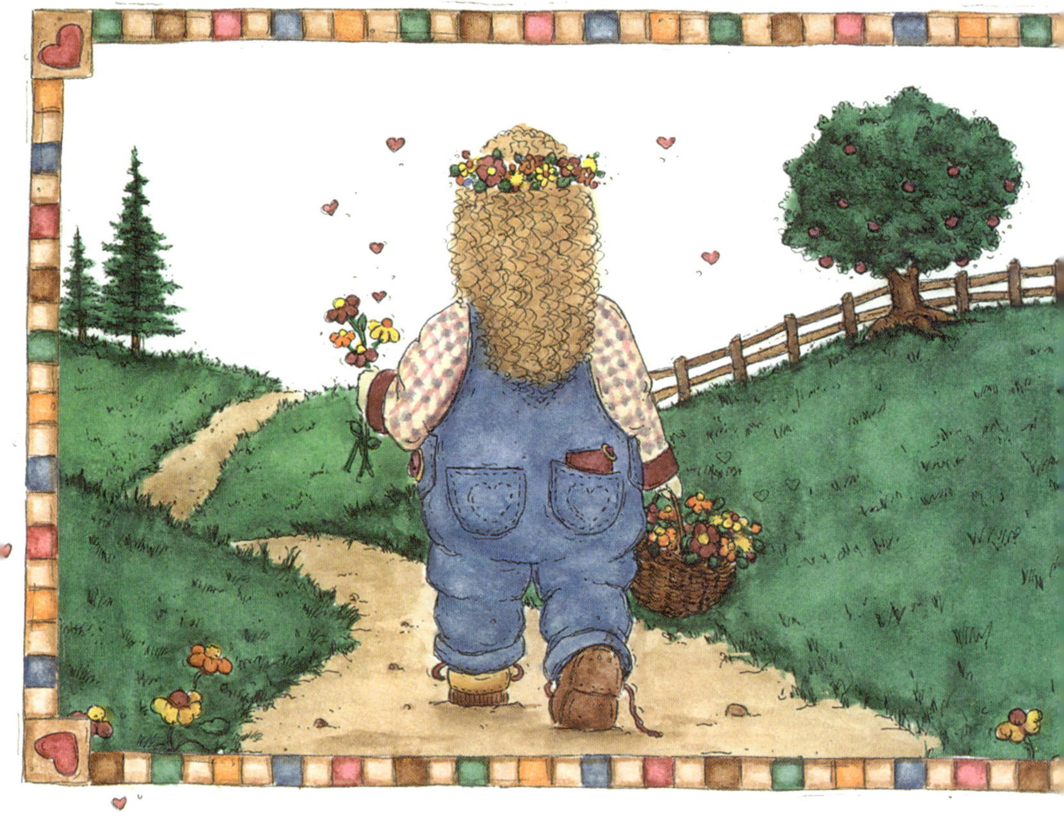

Natural Healing

We can learn much from the cycles of life in our beautiful world. Spending time outside, taking walks, lying in the cool grass, and even visiting a peaceful cemetery can heal us in ways only God understands.

It may be difficult to appreciate when your grief is new, but the wonder of God's world offers wisdom and serenity for your sorrowing heart.

Transformation Happens

    Our earthly bodies are like the cocoons that bind butterflies before they get their wings. Death is the transformation from our earthly state to the freedom and joy of eternal life.

    Your joy, too, is like a caterpillar within a cocoon. When grief and loss strike, you need time to withdraw, heal, and grow. Someday you will be ready to begin living and feeling again, and your joy will emerge in all the colorful splendor of the butterfly.

♥ Describe or draw your feelings within the cocoon of grief.

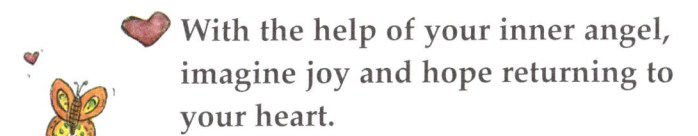

♥ With the help of your inner angel, imagine joy and hope returning to your heart.

Star Light, Star Bright

If you could wish on a star, you might wish for your life to be as it was before your loved one died. Though the sparkling heavens cannot work that miracle, the magic of a still, starry night can bring comfort to your heart.

Stand atop a hillside beneath a star-filled sky. You and your loved one are part of the same wonderful universe. Share your awe with your inner angel. Welcome the glimmer of joy back into your life.

You and your loved one
are part of the same
wonderful universe.

Heavenly Music

The Bible makes frequent mention of the angels' singing. Music is the language of faith and spirituality, and it helps us heal.

Whether you listen to sacred music, classical symphonies, or your loved one's favorite popular songs, the melodies and lyrics can open your heart to memories of brighter days. If the music brings tears and wistfulness, allow your inner angel to help you cherish the sadness as a part of your healing journey.

♥ Find and play a recording of your loved one's favorite song.

♥ How do you feel when you hear that special music?

Dare to Be Happy!

Joy

As you continue to work through your grief and look for the joy that remains, a day will come when you'll feel better. This rediscovered joy might seem frightening to you. After all, your grief has kept you connected to your loved one.

Your inner angel can help you believe that feeling good is not a betrayal of your loved one's memory. Nothing, not even healing and recovery from your grief, can take away the special relationship you've shared.

What's Good for the Body Is Good for the Soul

Have you neglected your physical well-being during your time of grief? The benefits of a healthy lifestyle are emotional as well as physical. Recovering from your grief and living each day to the fullest is a tribute to your loved one's memory.

The angel in you can keep you on track with your personal wellness. Wouldn't your loved one want it that way?

This One's for You!

♥ What are some lifestyle changes you've thought of making?

♥ Dedicate these changes—and the improved quality of life they represent—to your loved one's memory.

Thank God for your Loved One

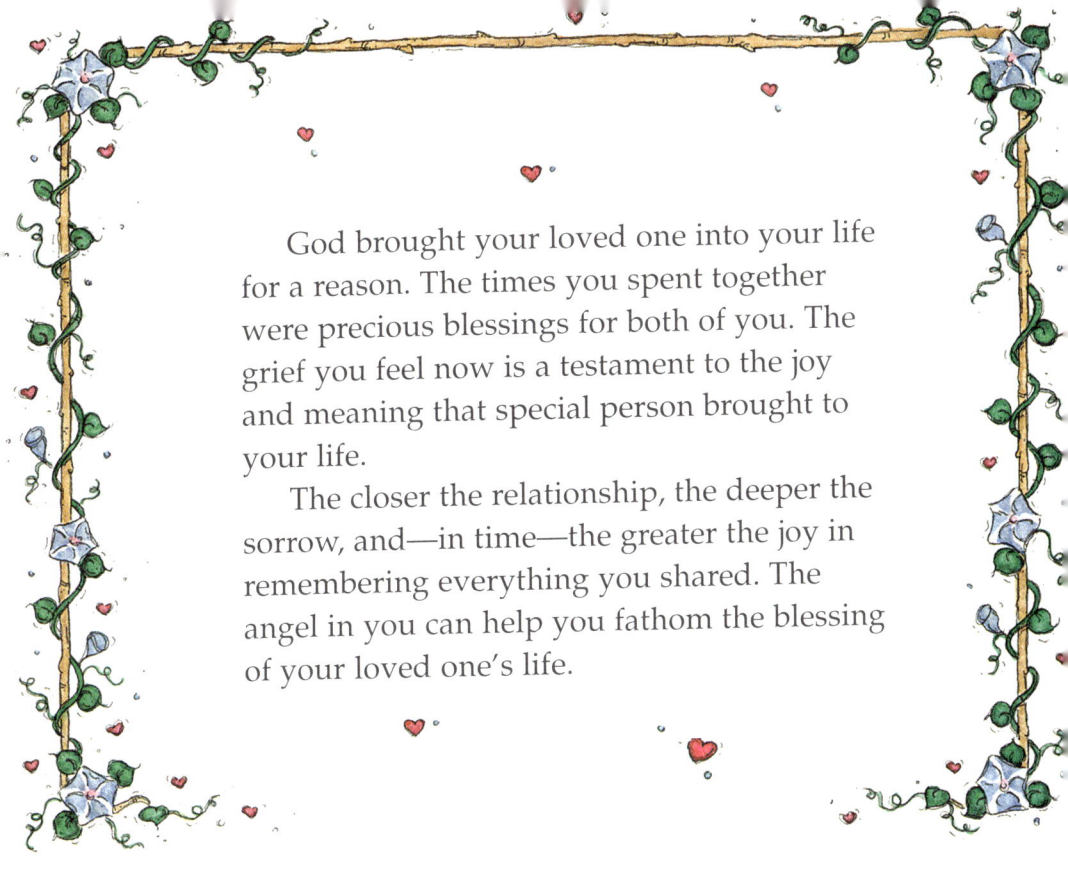

God brought your loved one into your life for a reason. The times you spent together were precious blessings for both of you. The grief you feel now is a testament to the joy and meaning that special person brought to your life.

The closer the relationship, the deeper the sorrow, and—in time—the greater the joy in remembering everything you shared. The angel in you can help you fathom the blessing of your loved one's life.

Love Lessons

We seldom realize how much joy people bring to us until they're gone. It may take months or even years to understand the depth of a loved one's impact on our lives.

As you honor the spirit and pass along the special gifts of your loved one, you become a living memorial to the meaning of that person's life.

Ask your inner angel to help you learn from your grief—to value the gifts and lessons you receive from every person along the way.

Life as Art

- List some of the ways your loved one touched your life. Think of symbols for each of these gifts.

- Make a drawing, sculpture, or collage illustrating your relationship with your loved one. Keep your work of art as a reminder of how you can pass along his or her memory to others in your life.

Remembering eases the pain

Loving support needed

Charity

Give Yourself (and Others) a Break

Your friends and family are searching for ways to help you—though some of their expressions of sympathy and offers of help may sound clumsy or insensitive. Keep in mind that not everyone has experienced profound loss, and that "people skills" are not all created equal.

Others may hesitate to talk with you about your loved one, fearing it may cause more tears and grief. Explain to them that knowing others remember makes your pain easier to bear. Allow your inner angel to help you ask for the loving support you need.

If There's Anything I Can Do...

    Be grateful for each compassionate offer of help from those around you. Now is the time to depend on others.

    Be willing to accept help with meals, laundry, child care, and cleaning. Freeing yourself from these tasks (which probably seem huge right now) gives you time to nurture yourself and to do the grieving you need to do.

♥ Who's offered to help you?

♥ What are some tasks they could help with?

Take time to nurture yourself.

The Wounded Healer

Grief, though painful and traumatic, can make positive changes in your life. Those who've experienced sorrow and turmoil are better equipped to comfort others going through difficult times.

The angel in you helps you learn from each difficult step of your grieving, as God gives you wisdom and peace to pass along to others.

Whether you choose to volunteer in a structured setting or simply vow to treat other human beings with renewed compassion, God can transform your grief into comfort offered to others.

God can transform your grief.

Share Wisdom and Guidance

Volunteer

Comfort Others

A Legacy of Love

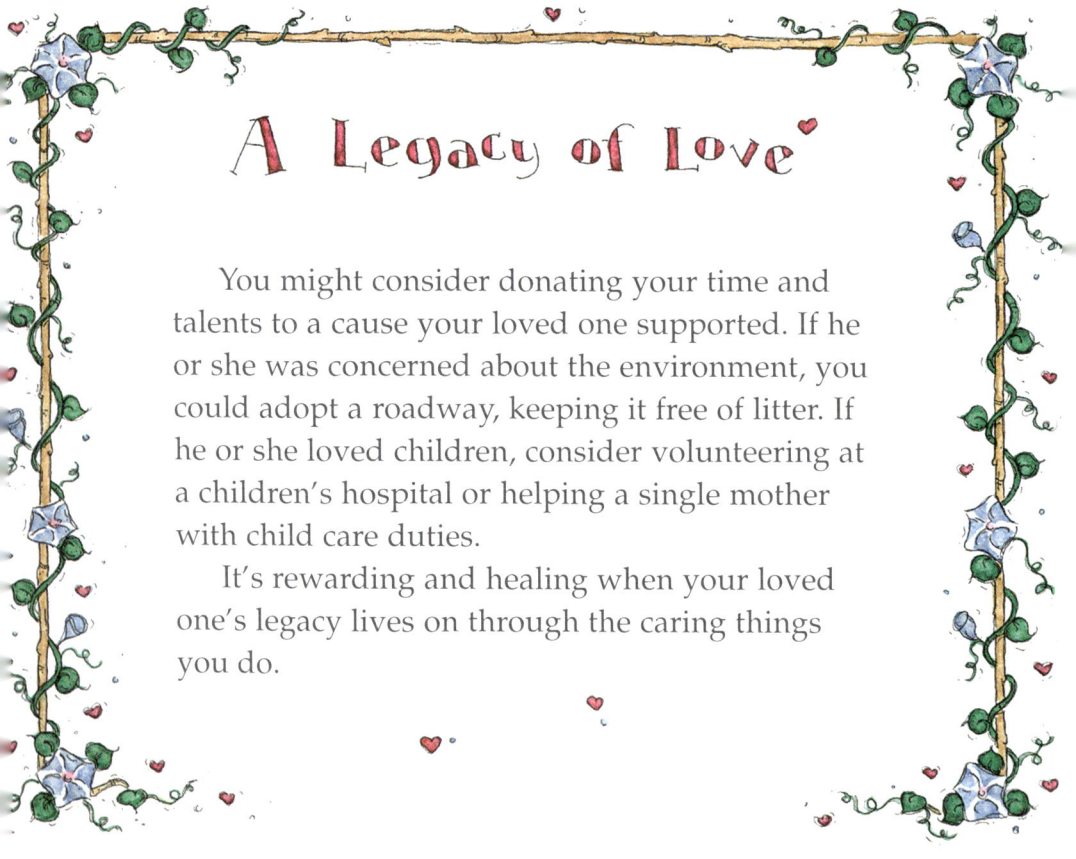

You might consider donating your time and talents to a cause your loved one supported. If he or she was concerned about the environment, you could adopt a roadway, keeping it free of litter. If he or she loved children, consider volunteering at a children's hospital or helping a single mother with child care duties.

It's rewarding and healing when your loved one's legacy lives on through the caring things you do.

♥ What was your loved one's pet cause or passion?

♥ What can you do to help?

Honor your loved one's legacy.

Peace Be With You

Hope

Though you'll continue to miss your loved one, strive to find comfort in God's promise of everlasting peace. Whether your loved one's death was sudden or the result of a lengthy illness, he or she is now experiencing freedom from the trials and pain of earthly life.

Through prayer and patience, joy and hope will one day ease the sorrow that now fills your heart.

Thank Heavens for Heaven!

Do you believe that "heaven" means pearly gates, harps, and angels? Is it a spiritual state of peace and serenity? Whatever your idea of heaven, try to visualize your loved one living in eternal comfort and happiness.

Your inner angel can help you move beyond despair to hope in the promise of heaven, and faith in the knowledge that your loved one is now at peace with God.

❤ **What is your idea of heaven? Draw or describe it here.**

People who have had near-death experiences describe loved ones helping them make the transition from the earthly world to life after death. Imagine your loved one's journey to heaven. Who do you think was there to welcome him or her? Imagine how you'll feel being greeted by your loved one when your time on earth is through.

Good Grief?

Memories

Grief is a lifelong process. The pain may subside and waves of sorrow may overtake you less often, but you'll always miss the presence of that special person in your life.

God created all your emotions, and each of them has a purpose in your life. In time, as your turmoil and despair lessen, you'll appreciate grief for keeping you close to your loved one in heart and memory.

Love Lives On!

You may recognize your loved one's essence in the gestures, expressions, or actions of others close to you. You may feel his or her presence each time you witness an act of kindness or compassion. You may experience the beauty of his or her life in the opening of a rosebud, the cry of an infant, or the splendor of a sunset.

Each of these reminders of your loved one's life is a precious gift from God. Be thankful for the opportunity to have known and loved such a remarkable person.

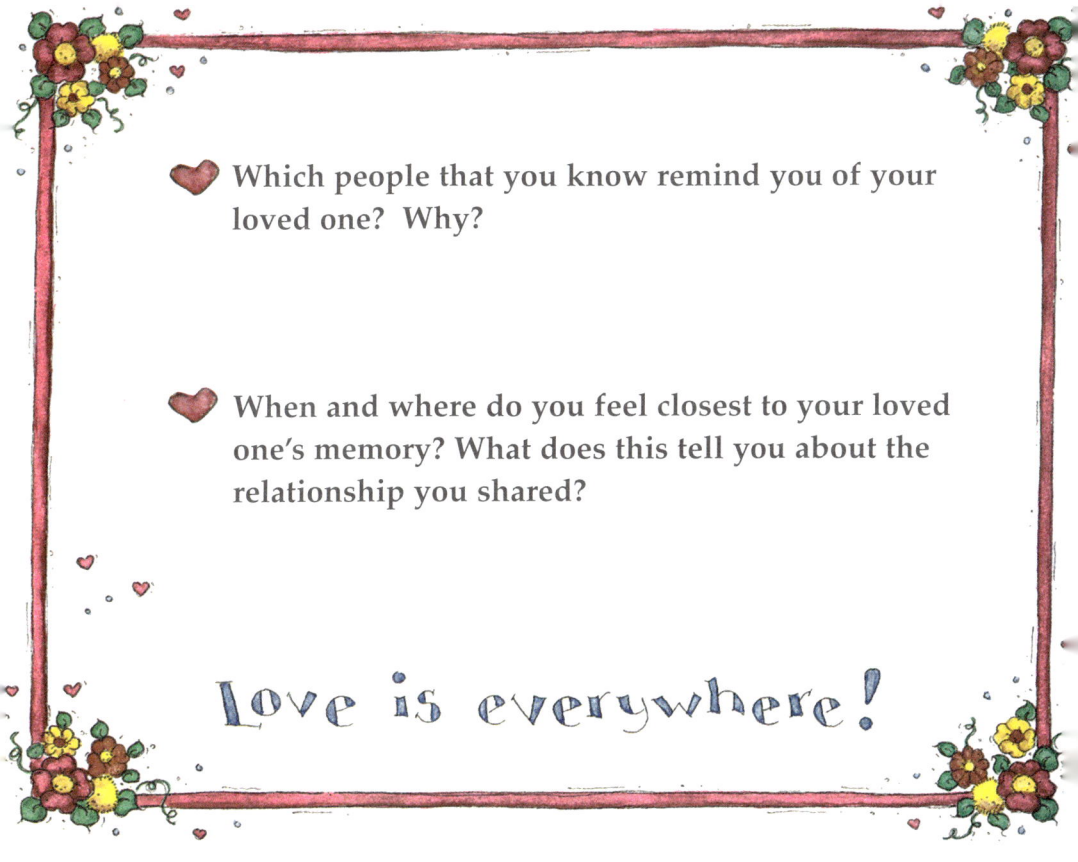

♥ Which people that you know remind you of your loved one? Why?

♥ When and where do you feel closest to your loved one's memory? What does this tell you about the relationship you shared?

Love is everywhere!

Help God Help You

The simple ideas in this book (or any book) may not always be enough to turn around an especially bad time. When your burden or grief overwhelms you, seek the help of a friend, physician, clergyperson, or counselor.

God wants us all to be happy.

Your Angel understands
Believe
Hope
Harmony
God bless the Angel in You
Faith
Charity
Joy
Grace

Your inner angel is always there to help you. When you feel alone, overwhelmed, or exhausted, your angel can give you strength. And your grief will eventually give way to a new sense of meaning and joy.

Through the guidance of God, caring people, and your own inner angel, you can grow through grief and transform it into a positive force in your life. God bless the angel in you!

❤ **Draw a picture of your angel and you.**

About the Heavenly Ways Books

Once upon an idea, in a little heartland village, an artist named Deb Haas Abell toiled away with her paintbrush and paints. Inspired by the many angels in her own life, she created six heart-sprinkling characters: Faith, Hope, Charity, Joy, Harmony, and Grace. Their one mission in life was to spread the message that God gives each of us the ability to be an angel on earth...to touch lives, lighten hearts, and inspire souls.

These warmhearted spirits began to share their heavenly message through gift and greeting products in

Abbey Press's Angel in You collection. Before long, they were introduced to writer Molly Wigand, who translated their wisdom into books like this one—about Heavenly Ways to cope, even in the midst of life's hardships and heartaches.

But this is not just another pretty fairy tale. For Faith, Hope, Charity, Joy, Harmony, and Grace are present every day inside each one of us! May these books help you to discover your own inner angel...and may God bless the angel in you!

Heavenly Ways Books

Heavenly Ways to Handle Stress
Heavenly Ways to Heal From Grief and Loss
Heavenly Ways to Grow Closer as a Family
Heavenly Ways to Find Your Own Serenity

Available at your favorite bookstore or directly from:
One Caring Place, Abbey Press Publications,
St. Meinrad, IN 47577.
Phone orders: (800) 325-2511.